How to
BEGIN your
JOURNEY with
MEDICARE

IMPORTANT PREPARATION STEPS
TO GET YOU ON THE RIGHT PATH!

BRIDGING THE INFORMATION GAP

by EDWARD NORRIS

SPIDER BOOKS
PUBLISHING

While the author has made every effort to provide accurate information and website addresses at the time of publication, neither the publisher nor the author assumes any responsibility for errors, for changes that occur after publication, or additional information. Updated information can be seen on the website at http://www.mediaapdecisions.com.

How to Begin Your Journey with Medicare
Important Preparation Steps to Get You on the Right Path
Bridging the Information Gap

Copyright © 2014, 2016 by Edward Norris

This book may be ordered through booksellers or by contacting:

Spider Books Publishing, LLC
2968 Ribbon Ct
Fort Myers, FL 33905
www.SpiderBooksPublishing.com
(239) 693-DRAW (3729)

ISBN: 978-0-9916538-6-7 (Print)
ISBN: 978-0-9916538-7-4 (Digital)

Printed in the United States of America

Editing, Cover & Book design: Jennifer FitzGerald - www.MotherSpider.com

TABLE OF CONTENTS

PREFACE

Are you baffled and frustrated by the application process for Medicare?

Even after 30 years of experience in health-care finance and compliance, I found the system puzzling and the available information difficult to sift through, especially when I tried to apply the general information running rampant in how-to books and articles to my specific circumstances. But I realized that if the process was challenging to navigate for me, it was probably overwhelming for others.

How to Begin Your Medicare Journey is the result of this experience, my career in health care, and months of detailed research, offering a narrative map explaining eligibility, application, available plans, the need for supplemental insurance, and the impact of new healthcare laws. Rather than just a dump of information, facts, and statistics, it offers clear, current data as well as guidance, creating the ultimate primer for applying for and utilizing Medicare.

The result is a sense of empowerment over your healthcare future and an understanding of a complicated system, streamlining your application process while providing you with the knowledge necessary to make informed decisions at every turn.

Concise and thorough, How to Begin

Your Medicare Journey answers the most pertinent questions surrounding this new stage in life, all without stress or confusion. Contact me today for a copy or learn more at http://www.MedigapDecisions.com

- Edward Norris

INTRODUCTION

One of my favorite quotes from Albert Einstein is

"I never teach my pupils. I only attempt to provide the conditions in which they can learn."

Although this is not a science class, there are some very important Medicare things to learn. I hope by providing you the following information you will gain some helpful insights in starting your Medicare journey.

My message is mainly for you baby boomers; to those of you who are about to reach your 65th birthday. Although Medicare is available for those under 65 with certain permanent disabilities, those having End Stage Renal Disease (ESRD), and those diagnosed as having Amyotrophic Lateral Sclerosis (ALS, or better known as Lou Gehrig's disease), the following suggestions are for you senior Americans.

As most of you already know, Medicare is a government health care coverage program governed by the Federal Government. Depending the choices that you make, your health care will be basically covered directly by the Federal Government, or by private insurance companies contracted with the Federal Government.

Sometimes people confuse Medicaid with Medicare. Please do not. Medicaid is for those people with limited income and resources. Medicaid is governed by each state with funding provided by both the Federal Government and the States. Later I'll discuss how Medicaid fits in with Medicare.

Also you need to know that some of Medicare is not free even though you paid your payroll taxes during your working life. And you need to know that you have some choices to make when you enroll. I'll mention choices a lot throughout this book.

I hope you will read this book before enrolling and before you seek out an insurance company or plan. By doing so you will become better informed about your Medicare and related choices. Also by taking this advice and information you will be in a leadership role, not depending on any media advertising to pressure you into making your choices.

There are no insurance products recommended in this book other than suggesting that you contact an independent insurance agent (or agents) in your area to obtain a variety of quotes from different insurance companies. If you need help in finding an agent, you can do a web search by keying in "Independent Insurance Agents & Brokers of (name your State) for Medicare".

You may already have, or soon will be receiving the Federal Government's book, Medicare & You, 2016, http://www.medicare.gov/Pubs/pdf/10050.pdf. It provides a lot of detailed information on Medicare, including enrollment, coverage, plan choices for your area, and a whole lot more.

I have attempted to mention the important Medicare highlights that will give you a basis on which to build if you so choose. There are lots of printed material, websites and videos that you can look up to read or view as you do your own investigation. Included throughout this book are various recommended websites, video links, and references from other sources to assist you in further research if you so desire.

Obviously not every one of your concerns will be addressed or covered. If you have specific questions, or have any exceptions to any item addressed in this book, please go to my website, (http://medigapdecisions.com/) to post them. I will answer, or clarify them on our Frequency Asked Questions (FAQ) page.

The information contained in this book are changed often, thus we plan to have updates to this book as new information becomes available. If you have purchased this book through a site other than my own, please visit my site and leave your email. When we update the book contents, you will receive a new digital version for FREE.

AM I ELIGIBLE FOR MEDICARE?

Most baby boomers are eligible. If you are already receiving Social Security (SS), you are definitely eligible to become a Medicare beneficiary (also those receiving Railroad Retirement Benefits, but I will be referring primarily to those SS eligible). Or if you have earned at least 40 work credits of Social Security, you are eligible for Medicare. People are usually enrolled automatically. Your Medicare card is mailed to you about three months before your 65th birthday.

For those of you who are not yet receiving your SS and are waiting until full retirement age of 66, you also can be enrolled for Medicare. Even if you or your spouse are still working and have employer or union sponsored healthcare benefits, you can still be enrolled. However, you may want to opt out of Part B by following instructions accompanying your Medicare card. More detail will be provided on this later.

Also a person who has not worked enough calendar quarters can become eligible for Medicare through their spouse.

Lastly if none of the above qualifies you to be eligible for Medicare, you can pay a monthly premium, http://www.medicare. gov/your-medicare-costs/part-a-costs/part-a-costs.html (more on this later).

WHAT ARE THE DISTINCT PARTS OF MEDICARE?

Medicare has four distinct parts, namely Part A, Part B, Part C, and Part D, with each responsible for paying for different benefits, subject to different eligibility criteria and financing mechanisms, such as premiums, deductibles, co-insurance. Parts A and B together are most generally called "original Medicare". Your choices are minimal such as whether to enroll in Part B, and if so do you need a Medicare supplement, also called a medigap policy (more on this later).

However, you will probably want to spend some significant time evaluating Parts C and D, as there are more choices to make and while they are very helpful for you, they are more complicated.

PART A - ORIGINAL, OR TRADITIONAL MEDICARE

This covers medically necessary health care in a hospital. Your provider, or emergency department physician must by his/her admitting diagnosis indicate that you require an inpatient stay that is medically necessary. Then Medicare will pay for any surgery, ancillary services, drugs, etc, that will help you get better.

If you need further skilled care after a three-day inpatient stay in the hospital,

Medicare will also pay for care in a skilled nursing facility (SNF) up to 20 days with no co-pay, and another 80 days with a co-pay.

Also Hospice and Home Health coverage comes under Part A (see the Medicare & You, 2016 handbook - pages 38-39)

For the calendar year 2016, the Medicare Part A deductible is $1,288 for each episode of inpatient admission. That is, if you are re-admitted for the same diagnosis later on, you don't have to pay the deductible again. But if you are admitted again under a different diagnosis, you are required to pay the full deductible again, even though the events happened in the same year. This Part A deductible usually increases each calendar year and is based on Medicare's average cost of a one-day stay.

Co-pays under Part A coverage come into play after you have been an inpatient 60 days during an episode of care, or benefit period. Reaching this milestone is not that common as the average length of an inpatient hospital stay is less than six days.

There is no monthly premium for Part A, if you paid Social Security/Medicare taxes for at least ten years, or have earned the minimum 40 credits (one credit equals one quarter of employment) of Social Security. Otherwise in order to obtain Part A, you will need to pay a monthly premium, which for the year 2016 is $411. Certain other Medicare eligible individuals who have to pay the Part A premium qualify for a 45% reduction, or a premium of $226 per month for 2016. Medicare estimates slightly less than

700,000 Medicare enrollees will pay these full and reduced premiums in 2016.

PART B - ORIGINAL, OR TRADITIONAL MEDICARE

Think of this part as medical insurance for outpatient services, provider/doctor services, durable medical equipment (DME), and some preventive services (see the Medicare & You, 2016 handbook – pages 69, 70 summary). Here again in order to qualify for Medicare payment, these services (except preventive services) must be medically necessary, that is, prescribed by your provider with a matching diagnosis.

Included under this part is observation status. This is when you are admitted to a hospital bed with your physician monitoring your condition and doing tests to determine how sick you are. This can take up to 48 hours in which you will be occupying a bed. After this observation stay you may be either discharged or admitted as an inpatient. If you are discharged to a nursing home, Medicare will not pay for the nursing home stay, as the 3-day minimum inpatient stay was not met. Recently it seems more Medicare patients are experiencing this event, resulting in paying the nursing home out-of-pocket.

Part B is not free like Part A for most beneficiaries. If you choose to enroll in Part B, you will have a monthly premium. The Part B premium that you will pay represents 25% of the total premium cost based on the level of Medicare health related expenses in the previous year. For the calendar year 2016 the monthly premium is $121.80, but increases for higher wage earners, http://www.medicare.gov/your-medicare-costs/part-b-costs/part-b-costs.html. The highest premium in 2016 is $389.80 a month. For those who receive Social Security benefits, this monthly premium is deducted from the monthly Social Security benefit.

The Part B deductible is usually changed each calendar year. It increases to $166 in 2016.

Also for each service mentioned above except outpatient lab and preventive services, there is a 20% co-insurance, which is based on Medicare's allowable charge. However, if you receive an outpatient service in a Critical

Access Hospital (CAH), the co-insurance may be based on the actual hospital's charge, which is usually a lot higher than Medicare's allowable charges.

Hospitals, physicians, and other providers of Part A and Part B services are typically paid on a fee-for-service basis (each service or group of services provided to a patient is reimbursed through a separate payment) using different prospective payment systems (PPS) or fee schedules. Certain other services are paid on the basis of reasonable costs or reasonable charges.

PART C – MEDICARE ADVANTAGE

MEDICARE CONTRACTING WITH PRIVATE INSURANCE COMPANIES

This part of Medicare is what is called Medicare Advantage, and is an alternative to the original Parts A and B of Medicare. You can choose to enroll in Medicare Advantage, which consists of private health plans that receive capitated payments for providing health care coverage to its enrollees. Medicare

Advantage plans pay health care providers for health care goods and services furnished to their enrollees at prices negotiated between the plans and providers. There are more options from which to choose in Part C. In the year 2015 about 32% of Medicare beneficiaries throughout the country on average were enrolled in these private plans.

Your payment of the Part B monthly premium ($121.80, which is deducted from your Social Security check or bank direct deposit) is a requirement in belonging to a Medicare Advantage Plan.

Medicare Advantage plans, which are offered by private insurance companies approved by Medicare, must offer benefits covered under original Medicare, except hospice care.

Medicare Advantage plans usually offer health benefits, such as vision, hearing, dental, and/or health and wellness programs, beyond what is included in the original Medicare benefit package.

Medicare Advantage plans may charge a monthly premium to cover the health benefits they offer, although many do not. The average monthly premium for the year 2016 is $32.60. In addition to health benefits, Medicare Advantage plans generally offer Part D prescription drug coverage, for which they may charge an additional premium.

Cost Sharing

Medicare Advantage plans can require that you pay cost sharing when you receive medical services. Your cost sharing can be in the form of

- a deductible—the amount you pay for services before Medicare begins to pay; however, very few Medicare Advantage plans have deductibles.

- coinsurance—a percentage of the cost for a given service that you must pay; and

- copayments—the stated amount you must pay for a service.

Medicare provides a lot of guidance to the Medicare Advantage plans that should give you some satisfaction. For example, they allow these plans to have different cost sharing requirements than original Medicare Parts A & B. However, overall they cannot be more than that actuarially projected for beneficiaries in original Medicare. Also Medicare requires that Medicare Advantage plans establish annual out-of-pocket limits for its members. As a comparison, original Medicare Parts A & B do not have out-of-pocket maximums.

The following are the main types of Medicare Advantage Plans (distribution of enrollment is for the year 2015):

1. Health Maintenance Organization (HMO) Plans – 66% of Medicare Advantage Plans

2. Preferred Provider Organization (PPO) Plans – 26% of Medicare Advantage Plans

3. Private Fee-for-Service (PFFS) Plans – 4% of Medicare Advantage Plans

Other Plans, including Special Needs Plans (SNP), Medical Savings Account (MSA) Plans – 4% of Medicare Advantage Plans

HMO Plans

(Health Maintenance Organization)

An HMO is an organization that provides or arranges managed care for your health insurance in a network. It covers care rendered by those hospitals, providers, doctors and other professionals who have agreed by contract to treat you and their members in accordance with their guidelines and restrictions.

In most cases, you must select a primary

care physician (PCP) from a list of approved providers who then act as "gatekeepers" to coordinate all your basic health care needs. For instance, when you need to see a specialist, you most likely need to get the PCP's permission or referral before seeing the specialist.

Generally HMO's will not cover your visits to doctors or hospitals outside the network except when you are traveling or have an emergency.

It is the most restrictive of the Medicare Advantage plans because almost all the healthcare HMO's have a pre-approval for treatment requirement. However, HMO's usually have the lowest premiums.

PPO Plans

(Preferred Provider Organization)

A PPO is a type of health insurance network arrangement allowing you the freedom to choose your own hospitals, doctors and other professionals. They negotiate with these providers to set fee schedules.

PPO's may also offer more flexibility than HMO's by allowing for visits to out-of-network providers, but at usually higher deductibles and higher co-payments than in-network.

Unlike an HMO, you are not required to select a primary care physician. However, some companies began on January 1, 2014, requiring a primary care physician to be listed on the application. You do not have to obtain a referral for a specialist.

If you go out-of-network for a specialist, your out-of pocket costs will be higher than for an in-network specialist.

Similar to HMO's, non-emergency hospital visits and outpatient surgery often must be pre-approved by the PPO plan in order to be covered.

PFFS PLANS
(Private Fee-for-Service)

This type of Medicare Advantage plan is almost like original Medicare, except that private insurance companies provide coverage. Some PFFS plans have contracted with network providers. This type of plan was the first Medicare Advantage plan offered, and since other types of plans are now available, it may be phased out.

Like original Medicare you can go to any Medicare approved doctor, hospital, or other healthcare provider that accepts the PFFS plan's payment. If these providers are out-of-network, you may pay more. A note of caution: providers have the ability to accept or not accept a PFFS plan on a case-by-case basis.

Medicare does not set the plan's payment to providers. The plan determines how much the providers are paid and how much is your share.

SNP's
(Special Needs Plans)

This is an exclusive Medicare Advantage plan. A law passed in 2003 identified special needs individuals limited to the following:

- Institutionalized – those residing in a long term facility
- Dually Eligible – Medicare with Medicaid
- Chronic Conditions – one or more disabling chronic condition

SNP's are designed to meet the special medical needs of these vulnerable groups of Medicare beneficiaries.

Generally you are required to have a primary care doctor. Also in most cases you will be required to get a referral to see a specialist.

MSA PLANS
(Medical Savings Account)

A Medicare MSA is the most con-sumer driven of all the Medicare Advantage plans as well as original Medicare. You are empowered to make all your own healthcare decisions.

This type of Medicare Advantage plan is unique with several differences from other private Medicare health plans. One big dif-ference is that there is no premium. Another difference is a big deductible. Since this type of plan is quite complex, Medicare has provided a helpful guide in a PDF format for this plan on their website, http://www.medicare.gov/pubs/pdf/11206.pdf.

Like the plan name signifies, there is a savings account as part of this plan. When you enroll in a Medicare MSA, the plan sets up your savings account with their bank (see the guide for exceptions).

Plan deductible is higher than other Medicare Advantage plans. For the year 2015 the plan deductible was as high as $10,600. Since you cannot have drug coverage in this type of plan, you will need to join a prescription drug plan if you want drug coverage.

You can use any doctor, hospital, or other healthcare provider who accepts Medicare.

In order to pay the lowest amount, make sure you use those participating providers who accept Medicare's approved amount as payment in full.

When you sign up for this type of Medicare Advantage plan, the MSA plan will deposit funds into your MSA bank account. This amount is less than your annual deductible. Before full coverage begins you will have to pay from your MSA savings account and out-of-pocket for any healthcare services.

Only funds disbursed for approved medical expenses (Medicare Part A and Part B services) will count toward the plan's deductible. Once the deductible has been met, the plan pays 100% of any further services needed in that calendar year.

Any remaining funds in your MSA savings account at the end of the calendar year are yours. These funds can be added to the following year's deposit from the plan. You can use your savings account funds for unapproved medical expenses, but they will not count toward the deductible.

You are not taxed for these savings funds used for medical expenses. However, if any of these plan deposited funds are used for non-medical expenses, you will pay taxes and possible financial penalties.

To briefly summarize MSA plan costs, you will need to enroll in Medicare Part B, enroll in Part D for prescription drug coverage, and for any medical expenses pay the difference between the plan deductible and plan deposit.

Very few Medicare recipients enroll in this plan option. If you are considering it you probably should discuss with both an independent insurance agent and your CPA tax preparer.

OTHER MEDICARE ADVANTAGE INFORMATION

When a Medicare Advantage Plan offers a Medicare prescription drug plan, you cannot enroll in the Medicare Part D prescription drug program. (more on this later)

To give you an idea what the Medicare Advantage plan premium cost is, the average monthly premium charged in the year 2015 by Medicare Advantage Plans for health benefits, excluding premiums for prescription drug coverage, was about $32.00. Results were based on all plans, including plans (except MSA) that do not charge a premium.

To help you in deciding whether to consider Medicare Advantage, here are the more prominent additional benefits Medicare Advantage plans provided in 2011:

- Professional services benefits (may include screenings and immunizations beyond what original Medicare covers)
- 98% of Medicare Advantage Plans offered this additional benefit
- Health and education benefits (may include nutritional training, smoking cessation, health club memberships, or nursing hotlines
- 98% of Medicare Advantage Plans offered this additional benefit
- Inpatient facility benefits (may include

additional days beyond what original Medicare covers)

- 97% of Medicare Advantage Plans offered this additional benefit.
- International outpatient emergency benefits (may include additional services beyond what original Medicare covers)
- 97% of Medicare Advantage Plans offered this additional benefit.
- Outpatient blood benefits (may include payment associated with pints of blood received as an outpatient or as part of a Part B-covered service beyond what original Medicare covers)
- 91% of Medicare Advantage Plans offered this additional benefit
- Vision benefits (may include coverage for routine eye exams, contact lenses, or eyeglasses)

- 79% of Medicare Advantage Plans offered this additional benefit
- Skilled nursing facility benefits (may include waiving the 3-day inpatient hospital stay requirement in original Medicare)
- 68% of Medicare Advantage Plans offered this additional benefit
- Hearing benefits (may include coverage for hearing tests, hearing aid fittings, and hearing aid evaluations)
- 64% of Medicare Advantage Plans offered this additional benefit.
- Dental benefits (may include oral exams, teeth cleanings, fluoride treatments, dental X-rays, or emergency dental services)
- 38% of Medicare Advantage Plans offered this additional benefit

Medicare in 2008 established a Medicare Advantage rating system. It's called a star scale with a range of 1 (low rating) to 5 (high rating). You may use these ratings in combination with information about benefits, co pays, and available providers, to select the Medicare Advantage plan that best meets your needs.

PART D – PRESCRIPTION DRUG PLANS

This part of Medicare is known as the Prescription Drug Plan (PDP), a voluntary outpatient prescription drug benefit under Medicare Part D that was made effective January 1, 2006. Original Medicare Parts A and B basically do not cover outpatient prescription drugs. However, most Medicare Advantage Plans (Part C) will cover drugs.

Medicare prescription drug coverage is insurance provided by private companies that have been approved by Medicare and available to every Medicare beneficiary. Medicare contracts with private companies to offer this drug coverage. These companies offer a variety of options, with different covered prescriptions, different deductibles and co-insurance.

By having this Medicare drug coverage may help lower your prescription drug costs and help protect against higher drug costs in the future.

Joining a Medicare drug plan is optional. You aren't required to join a Medicare plan, and you should not join until you are sure how it would affect your current coverage, if any.

If you want to participate, you should

choose a plan offering the coverage that best meets your needs and then enroll. In most cases, there is no automatic enrollment to get a Medicare prescription drug plan.

You can get Medicare prescription drug coverage in the following ways:

- Through Medicare Advantage Plans (except MSA's), or other Medicare Health Plans that are offering coverage far prescription drugs.
- Through Medicare Prescription Drug Plans, which add coverage to Original Medicare, and
- Through some Medicare Cost Plans, and Medicare Private Fee-for-Service Plans.

Medicare has set a minimal standard for their prescription drug plan. All drug plans must provide coverage that is at least as good as this standard. Some plans might offer more coverage and additional drugs for higher monthly premiums. You can choose and join the Medicare drug plan that best suits your needs. Regardless of your choice, you will have to pay a monthly premium (there are exceptions, so more on this later).

If you decide not to join a Medicare drug plan when you are first eligible, you may have to pay a penalty if you decide to join later.

You can join a Prescription Drug Plan when you first become eligible for Medicare, called the Initial Enrollment Period. If you do not join during this period, you may have to pay a penalty, which lasts as long as you have your new Medicare prescription drug coverage.

The late enrollment penalty that is added to your Part D premium works like this. If after your initial enrollment period there is a period of more than 63 days you did not have creditable coverage, the government applies a monthly penalty of 1% of the "national base premium" ($33.13 in 2015) to your Part D premium.

So, if you go three years without the coverage and then decide to take advantage of enrolling in a plan, you will have a permanent penalty of $11.93 added to whatever your monthly premium will be for your coverage. (see the 2016 Medicare & You booklet – pages 112-113)

Other times for possible enrollment is during a Special Enrollment Period (SEP), then you may be able to join without paying a penalty:

- If you move out of your plan's service area.
- If you have both Medicare and Medicaid.
- If you qualify for Extra Help to pay for your prescription drug costs.
- If you live in a nursing home.

Although original Medicare Parts A and B do not cover prescription drugs, they do cover some drugs in certain cases such as immunosuppressive drugs for transplant patients and some oral anti-cancer drugs. Medicare also covers certain prescription drugs used in nebulizers and external infusion pumps.

If you plan to get Medicare covered prescription drugs, make sure your pharmacy or supplier is enrolled in the Medicare Program, otherwise Medicare will not pay. You will then be responsible for paying the entire bill. Under current law, all Medicare enrolled pharmacies must accept assignment for Medicare covered drugs and biologicals (that is, accept whatever Medicare pays).

Medicare prescription drug coverage is available to everyone with Medicare, regardless of your income and resources, health status, or current prescription expenses. If you enroll in the Medicare PDP when you first become eligible, you will not be required to show that you have credible coverage. This means that your current drug coverage is expected to pay, on average, at least as much as Medicare coverage. Should you decide to sign-up later you may incur a late enrollment penalty.

If you are still employed and have employer/union coverage you probably have creditable coverage. If so, they will provide a written notice indicating such. You can keep your employer/union coverage as long as it is still offered.

Keep a copy of this coverage notice. If you join a Medicare drug plan after you are first eligible, you will need to provide this notice as proof of coverage. Your plan may contact you for additional information. They will determine whether you have had continuous creditable drug coverage and send this information to Medicare.

Should you drop or lose your coverage there is no penalty:

- If you involuntarily lose the coverage, but you must join a Medicare drug plan with an effective date that is within 60 days of the coverage end date.
- If you chose to drop the coverage, you must join a Medicare drug plan within 3 months of dropping the coverage. However, if you do not enroll in a Medicare drug plan and have a period of 63 days or longer without creditable coverage, you will have to pay a penalty when you eventually do enroll.
- If your current employer/union coverage is non-creditable, here are some options you might be able to take:
- Keep your current employer/union drug plan and join a Medicare drug

plan that gives you more complete coverage.

- Keep only your current employer/ union drug plan. If you join a Medicare drug plan after you are first eligible, you will incur a penalty.

- Drop your current coverage and join a Medicare drug plan or a Medicare Advantage drug plan.

- If you drop your employer/union coverage, you may not be able to get it back. You may not be able to drop your employer/union drug coverage without also dropping your employer/ union health coverage.

In some cases, employers or unions have rules that say you cannot have both a Medicare drug plan and your employer/union plan. So then by enrolling in a Medicare drug plan, your current coverage may end for you and your dependents.

You should talk to your employer/union and/or the benefits administrator about all of your options.

If you are covered under COBRA, you should check with your former employer/ union or the benefits administrator to see if the coverage is creditable.

Workers' compensation, discount drug card programs, and manufacturer patient assistance programs (PAPs) are not considered creditable coverage.

As mentioned earlier, when you get Medicare prescription drug coverage you pay a premium each month to join the drug plan.

Your premium, deductible, and co-insurance vary depending on which plan you choose. Some plans offer more coverage and/or vary the standard level of coverage by charging copayments based on drug tiers or lowering the deductible in exchange for higher out-pocket-costs later on.

There is also "extra help" (also called a "low-income subsidy", or LIS) to help people with Medicare who have limited income and resources to pay for Medicare prescription drug coverage. If you qualify for extra help, you will get help paying for your Medicare drug plan's monthly premium, and for some of the costs you would normally pay for your prescriptions. The amount of extra help you get will be based on your income and resources. You can apply for extra help by calling Social Security at 1-800-772-1213 or going to the Social Security website.

Most Medicare drug plans have a coverage gap, or a "donut hole" as some call it. This means that after you and your plan have spent a certain amount of money for covered drugs, you have to pay some of the costs out-of-pocket for your drugs (up to a limit).

The Explanation of Benefits notice, which your drug plan mails to you each month when you fill a prescription, will tell you how much you've spent on covered drugs and whether you've entered the coverage gap. To help you understand this Part D coverage gap, or "Donut Hole", the National Council on Aging (NCOA) provides an illustration on how this coverage works. You can download the document at their website: https://www.ncoa.org/resources/

donut-hole-the-medicare-part-d-coverage-gap-illustrated/. You can also read about the Medicare Part D coverage gap at the Medicare.gov website, http://www.medicare.gov/part-d/costs/coverage-gap/part-d-coverage-gap.html.

RETIREE DRUG COVERAGE

Your employer (or the plan that administers your retiree drug coverage) should provide a creditable coverage disclosure notice to you about how your retiree health or drug coverage will be affected if you join a Medicare plan. This information will also tell you how your retiree drug coverage compares to the Medicare prescription drug coverage.

If your retiree drug coverage will stay the same, and the coverage is creditable coverage, you can stay with your current coverage now, and you won't have to pay a penalty if you later decide to switch to Medicare drug coverage. However, if you qualify for extra help to pay for Medicare drug coverage, it is possible that you could get better coverage if you join a Medicare drug plan.

Read the information from your retiree plan carefully. It will help you understand your options. It should also tell you how to contact the plan if you have questions. If there is no information on whom to contact, contact your benefits administrator or the office that answers questions about your coverage.

WHAT ABOUT MY CURRENT PRESCRIPTIONS?

Medicare drug plans do not have to cover every drug that's included in Medicare prescription drug coverage. They only have to cover every type of drug. You should review what drugs are covered by the Medicare drug plans available in your area and try to join one that covers the same prescriptions you take now.

If the plan does not cover your exact prescriptions, the plan is required to have a transition period where your current drugs may be covered for a certain length of time while you work with your doctor to find an alternative prescription drug to take that is covered by the plan.

If your doctor believes you need to take your current prescription drug and should not switch to a covered prescription drug, you or your doctor can contact your plan and ask it to give you an "exception" which means the plan agrees to pay for your current drug. If the plan refuses to give you an exception, you can appeal the plan's decision.

However, if you are currently stabilized on certain specific prescription drugs (like drugs for depression, cancer or HIV/AIDS), you don't have to switch to a different prescription drug. Please talk to your doctor or pharmacist to see if your prescription drugs qualify.

When you join, the Medicare drug plan will send you information about its appeal procedures. Read the information carefully and call your plan if you have any questions.

HOW TO PAY MY PREMIUM

You have choices in the way you pay your Medicare drug plan premium. Depending on your plan and your situation, you may be able to pay your Medicare drug plan premium in one of four ways:

- Deducted from your checking or savings account.
- Charged to a credit or debit card.
- Billed to you each month directly by the plan. Some plans bill in advance

for coverage the next month. Send your payment to the plan, not Medicare. Contact your plan for the payment address.

- Although personally I do not recommend this payment method, you can, however, have your premium deducted from your monthly Social Security payment. Contact your drug plan (not Social Security) to ask for this payment option. With this option, your first deductions usually take 3 months to start, and 3 months of premiums will likely be collected at one time. You may also see a delay in premiums being withheld if you switch or leave plans, and may be unable to obtain your medications until Social Security completes the change.

Discounts

You may use a discount card or other pharmacy discount during your deductible period or while in the coverage gap. In some cases, a network pharmacy may accept a discount card or offer another cash price discount so that you can pay less for a prescription than your plan's negotiated price. This is considered a one-time "lower cash" or special price.

If you are able to obtain a cash discount to pay an amount that's lower than your plan's price, you will need to send your receipt to your Medicare drug plan. This ensures that your plan will count the amount you paid towards your out-of-pocket costs.

Medicare Prescription Drug Plans must include at least two drugs in every drug category. The plans must also do the following:

- Make sure you have convenient access to retail pharmacies;
- Have a process for you to get drugs that are not on the list of covered drugs (formulary) when it is medically necessary; and
- Provide useful information to you, such as how formularies and medication management programs work, information on saving money with generic drugs, and grievance and appeal processes.

Make a list of all your current medications, including name, dose size (for example- 2 pills, 300mg in each pill), dosage frequency (for example- 2 times a day) and monthly costs of your current prescriptions. You can use this information to compare the list of drugs (also called a formulary) that are covered under each plan. You can get the list of drugs a plan covers by calling the plan or by visiting the plan's website.

For more information, please visit Medicare's secured search tool, the Medicare Prescription Drug Plan Finder at this web site (copy and paste this URL to your web browser):

https://www.medicare.gov/find-a-plan/questions/home.aspx

Additional PDP Information

Each state that has a State Pharmacy Assistance Program (SPAP) will decide how its program will work with the Medicare drug coverage. Some states may choose to give extra coverage when you join a Medicare drug plan to assist with your out-of-pocket expenses. Some states may have a separate state program that helps with prescriptions. You should contact your SPAP for more information.

Certain drugs are excluded; which means they can't be provided as part of standard Medicare prescription drug coverage. Some examples of excluded drugs include benzodiazepines, barbiturates, drugs for weight loss or gain, and erectile dysfunction drugs. However, a plan can choose to cover excluded drugs if the plan offers more than standard coverage. Non-prescription drugs may be covered under certain circumstances at no cost.

Medicare is offering help to employers and unions to encourage them to keep providing high quality prescription drug coverage. If your employer or union is claiming you for the retiree drug subsidy, you should first talk to your benefits administrator before making any changes to your current coverage. If you try to join a Medicare drug plan, your benefits administrator and/or the Medicare drug plan may contact you to confirm your choice.

You may not be able to have both Medicare drug coverage and employer/retiree drug coverage if your employer is claiming you for the retiree drug subsidy. Your employer is responsible for telling you how their coverage works with Medicare.

The Medicare Prescription Drug Plan finder can provide pricing for prescription drugs but cannot provide pricing for over-the-counter drugs and diabetic supplies. Diabetic supplies are eligible to be covered under Part D. Medicare has provided this comprehensive document on Diabetic covered services (including supplies): http://www.medicare. gov/Library/PDFNavigation/PDFInterim.

asp?Language=English&Type=Pub&
PubID=11022

Regional drug plans will generally only cover prescriptions from pharmacies in a particular area. (Some prescriptions may be covered in other areas in an emergency.) There are national plans that cover prescriptions all over the country.

Medicare records reflect the beneficiary address of record at the Social Security Administration and this zip code should be used for the Medicare Prescription Drug Plan Finder. Around October before each Open Enrollment Period, or Annual Election Period, Medicare announces the Prescription Drug plans that offer national drug coverage. This information is available at the Open Enrollment Center, http://www.cms.gov/

center/special-topic/open-enrollment-center.
html?redirect=/center/openenrollment.asp
and may be of value for beneficiaries that
live in multiple areas of the United States
and territories throughout the plan year.

Medicare drug plans will include drugs
in all disease categories. They must also have
an appeals and exceptions process; which
must include ways to help people who have
trouble handling the process themselves.

Look for information about plans in your
area in the Medicare & You 2016 handbook,
Section 12.

Also the American Cancer Society website, http://www.cancer.org/treatment/find-
ingandpayingfortreatment/managingin-
suranceissues/medicare/medicarepartd/

medicare-part-d-getting-help-to-pay-for-medicare has a very good explanation of Medicare's Part D as it relates to cancer patients. It quite lengthy and I would highly recommend you download it, especially if you have cancer.

VETERANS ADMINISTRATION PRESCRIPTION DRUG COVERAGE

If you get VA health benefits, your coverage will not change. If you decide that VA drug coverage meets your needs, you can choose not to join a Medicare drug plan. You can keep your current coverage.

It will almost always be to your advantage to keep your current coverage without making any changes. An exception is if you qualify for Medicare's extra help. You may benefit by applying for the extra help.

VA prescription drug coverage is considered creditable drug coverage, which means VA expects to pay, on average, at least as much as Medicare drug coverage. If you decide you want to join a Medicare drug plan after you are first eligible, you won't have to pay a late enrollment penalty if you join within 63 days of involuntarily losing your VA coverage. If you don't lose your coverage and you want to join a Medicare drug plan, you must wait for a valid enrollment period. You will not have to pay a late enrollment penalty.

If you have VA coverage and you choose to dis-enroll from your Medicare drug plan, you get a special enrollment period to do so.

You should contact your local VA facility before making any changes to your drug coverage.

Based on your prescription drug needs, you may choose to have both VA and Medicare drug coverage.

If you are thinking about joining a Medicare drug plan and you have VA benefits, you should consider:

- Where you live:

You may benefit from Medicare drug coverage if you are in a nursing home that does not let you use your current VA drug benefits. You may also want Medicare drug coverage if you live far from a VA facility.

- Where you want to fill your prescriptions:

In most cases, with VA drug coverage, you must get your drugs from a VA pharmacy in person or by mail. If you'd rather get your prescriptions from local retail pharmacies, you may want to consider a Medicare drug plan.

For additional information, please contact the VA Health Benefits Service Center at 1-877-222-8387.

How and When do I Enroll in Medicare?

Perhaps you are thinking, since you paid into the Social Security/Medicare Program during your earnings years that being covered by Medicare would be automatic. Well sort of, but you still must sign-up as there are choices to make. Once you enroll you do not have to enroll each year, but you may make some changes (see last chapter).

If you are already receiving Social Security benefits as early distribution, you will automatically be enrolled in Part A. Medicare will send you a Medicare card before your 65th birthday. After receiving it you may need to make a choice.

If you are not receiving Social Security benefits yet, you can sign-up for these Part A benefits by visiting your nearest Social Security office, or logging on the Social Security website: https://www.socialsecurity.gov/planners/retire/justmedicare.html

Even though you may still be working and having good health coverage benefit, I suggest that you sign-up as early as possible.

The earliest you can enroll in Part A is three months before the month you turn 65. For instance, if your 65th birthday is in July, you can sign-up as early as April 1, and your Part A benefits become effective July 1. However, since your initial enrollment period is seven months long, you can wait to sign up as late as the third month past your birthday month, and in this case would be October 31. Benefits will also start later, usually the first of the following month of sign-up.

Another thing to keep in mind as you think through this enrollment process depends on whether you are still working for a large employer who is providing group healthcare coverage. In this case as you enroll you may want to decline signing up for Part B. Since you are probably paying part of your group premium (most employees do), why would you need to enroll in Part B and begin paying a monthly premium of at least $121.80?

If you decide not to enroll in Part B

because you have group coverage provided by your employer or union, you can also wait until the earliest when

(a) your employment ends, or

(b) your coverage ends.

In this case Medicare provides an eight-month Special Enrollment Period (SEP) for you. It begins the month after employment termination or the end of your employer coverage.

For example, if your employment terminates in January, then you have February through September to enroll in Medicare Part B (in this instance let's assume you already had enrolled in Part A).

As mentioned earlier, Part D enrollment

is voluntary. If you decide to enroll in this Prescription Drug Program, you should do it the same time you enroll in Parts A and B, or a Medicare Advantage plan without drug coverage.

WHAT HAPPENS IF I DON'T SIGN UP WHEN FIRST ELIGIBLE?

Either at age 65, or during the Special Enrollment Period?

Part A is premium free, provided that you paid your appropriate Medicare taxes while working, or are eligible through a spouse. For some of you who did not pay enough Medicare taxes, Part A premium payment is required to participate in Part A. In this case if you did not enroll in Part A when you first become eligible, you may incur a 10% premium penalty for each 12-month period delay in enrollment. This penalty is added to the premium for each month as long as you have Medicare.

Since Parts B and D have premiums, anyone not signing-up at age 65, or during the SEP, there is also a 10% penalty for each 12-month delay that is added to your monthly premium. For instance, if you delay enrolling for Part B in the year, 2015, the year you turned 65 and ended employment, and you plan to enroll in the year 2018, your penalty may be 20% (add the 10% for year 2016 to the 10% for the year 2017). Like the Part A penalty, this Part B penalty is added to each monthly premium as long as you have Part B.

Do I Need Additional Insurance to Medicare?

That depends on whether you choose to go with original Medicare Part A and Part B, or with a Medicare Advantage Plan.

Like was stated above there are deductibles and co-insurance costs with both original Medicare and Medicare Advantage Plans. Only beneficiaries having original Medicare are eligible to obtain additional coverage for these deductibles and co-insurances. Medicare Advantage beneficiaries do not need, nor can they be sold supplemental insurance coverage.

There are different types of supplemental insurance, including medigap, retiree insurance, and income based programs. How supplemental insurance coordinates with Medicare depends on the plan. The type of coverage that we will discuss is called Medicare supplement, or medigap insurance sold by private insurance companies.

If you decide on original Medicare and are enrolling in both Part A and Part B, you have the option to buy this medigap insurance coverage. Depending on where you live, you have up to 10 different medigap plans, or policies (A, B, C, D, F, G, K, L, M, N) to choose from. Three States, Massachusetts, Minnesota, and Wisconsin standardize medigap plans differently.

The first step is to decide whether you want this supplemental coverage. Next you will need to find out which plans or policies are available to be sold in your state, http://www.medicare.gov/find-a-plan/questions/medigap-home.aspx. Not all plans are available in all areas.

As you review these supplemental insurance companies, please keep in mind their A.M. Best Company rating. You will want to choose an insurance company that rates at least an A or a B. The better the rating the more financial viable the company is. And you definitely want the company to be around for a while. Or you can go to the Weiss Ratings website for their rating of insurance companies. You will need to register before accessing their website for a ratings search.

When you have a claim Medicare pays first and then the medigap plan usually has a crossover agreement with Medicare that allows them to automatically pay any deductible and/or co-pay.

Each medigap plan pays for a particular set of benefits. Plan A offers the fewest benefits and is usually the least expensive. Plans that offer more benefits, like Plan F, are generally more expensive. The most popular medigap plans are C, G, and F, because they cover major benefits and are less expensive than many other plans.

For instance, take a look at Plan G. It offers the same coverage as Plan F, but has a $166.00 deductible for the year. However, the annual premium saved by taking advantage of Plan G compared to Plan F will save you more money in premium than the $166.00 you will pay in the deductible. Because Plan F is the only plan offered with guaranteed coverage, costs are increasing more than the other plans. The differences between the plans are not the benefits offered, but solely the costs and the service you receive from the company you select. There are only two times that you may exercise a guaranteed issue: (1) if you lose your employer retirement plan, or (2) if your Medicare Advantage plan is discontinued.

Under national law, you only have the right to buy a medigap policy at certain times. All states must give people with Medicare, at minimum, the purchase protections offered under federal law.

A few states, like New York and Connecticut, give you much broader protections. It is important to know when you have the right to buy a medigap policy. If you miss your window of opportunity, your costs may go up or insurers may refuse to sell you any medigap at all.

For exact rules and protections in your state, contact your State Health Insurance Assistance Program (SHIP) or your state's Department of Insurance.

At times when you have the right to buy a medigap policy, an insurance company cannot

- deny you medigap coverage; or
- charge you more for a policy because of past or present health problems.

If it is not a time when you have the right to buy a medigap policy, you may still be able to buy a plan if a company is willing to sell you one. However, companies are not required to sell you a medigap policy. If they are willing to sell a medigap policy to you, they can charge you a higher price.

A pre-existing condition is a condition or illness that you were diagnosed with or got treatment for before your new health care coverage began.

Under national laws, you may have up to a six-month waiting period for medigap coverage of pre-existing conditions unless you are in one of the following situations:

You are entitled to a guaranteed-issue right to buy a medigap policy because you recently lost certain types of other coverage;

You purchased a medigap policy during an open enrollment period and had coverage from one of the following types of insurance for at least six months prior to purchasing the medigap policy and have had this prior coverage within the last 63 days:

Medicare Parts A and B

- Private health insurance coverage (including Medicare private health plans)
- Group health plan (like an employer plan)
- COBRA
- Medicaid
- CHAMPUS AND TRICARE (health care programs for the uniformed

military services)

- Federal Employees Health Benefit Program
- A public health plan
- State health benefits risk pool
- Indian Health Service or Tribal Organization Program
- A health plan under the Peace Corps Act
- Veterans Administration benefits

If you had no previous health insurance coverage or you did, but you waited more than 63 days after it ended to buy a medigap policy, the company can make you wait up to six months for coverage for health problems you already have.

If you are replacing a medigap policy you have had for at least six months with a new medigap policy, you will have no pre-existing condition waiting period for those benefits covered by your old plan. However, you may have a waiting period of any new benefits in the new plan you choose.

Not all plans impose pre-existing condition waiting periods. If you do not have coverage that is considered creditable, shop around to find a plan that does not make you wait for coverage of services to treat your preexisting conditions and offers coverage at an affordable price.

According to the Department of Veterans Affairs Health Administration Center, CHAMPVA (Civilian Health and Medical Program of Department of Veteran Affairs) benefits are available to those veterans over age 65. If you are a veteran, a spouse of a veteran, or a widow(er) of a veteran, you might want to check if you are eligible. Please visit the Veterans Affairs website for more information, https://www.ebenefits.va.gov/ebenefits/CHAMPVADashboard

To help in your decision whether to go with original Medicare and a medigap plan, or go with Medicare Advantage, Consumer Reports has a chart that I find helpful. http://www.consumerreports.org/cro/news/2013/11/comparing-medigap-and-medicare-advantage/index.htm

Many current Medicare beneficiaries who have original Medicare and a supplemental plan have indicated to me that they like these coverages because it's easier to budget. They know how much is being taken from their social security each month for Part B, and exactly how much their medigap premium is each month.

Are My Choices Permanent?

The short answer is no.

After you make your initial decision to enroll in Medicare you can still change your decision, but only at certain times of the year. You get a chance at least annually to reevaluate that initial decision and make a change if you so desire. This period of time is called the Open Enrollment season which runs from October 15 and December 7.

If you are in a Medicare Advantage plan and have decided that original Medicare is the better option, you can make this change within 45 days of enrolling in the Medicare Advantage plan. You can also make this change during the October 15 and December 7 period.

There is a disenrollment period from January 1 through February 15 each year allowing you to return to Medicare and pick up a Medicare supplement and/or a stand-alone PDP.

If you initially enrolled in original Medicare you can change and select a Medicare Advantage plan offered in your area during this October 15 and December 7 period.

If you are enrolled in Part D but want to change to a different plan, you must wait until the annual October 15 and December 7 period.

However, there is now a 5-Star special enrollment period from December 8, 2015 to November 30, 2016. If you are not in a 5-Star Medicare Advantage Plan, or Prescription Drug Plan, you can switch to a 5-Star Plan during this time frame.

Does Obamacare impact Medicare?

It certainly does, but not in the sense of how to enroll or make premium payments. Obamacare is a comprehensive health care reform bill, which is made up of two laws:

Patient Protection and Affordable Care Act, (PPACA) which was signed into law on March 23, 2010. And then it was amended by the Health Care and Education Affordability Reconciliation Act of 2010 (HCERA), which was signed into law on March 30, 2010.

Some people call these laws collectively Obamacare or Health Reform Law (HRL).

Obamacare, or Health Reform Law, makes several changes to the Medicare program, but probably not that evident to most Medicare beneficiaries. It contains numerous provisions affecting Medicare payments to certain providers, payment rules for Medicare Advantage plans, covered benefits, and the delivery of care. In addition there are new Medicare taxes on high wage earners and on net investment income.

The Health Reform Law changes maximum payments to Medicare Advantage plans. The phase-in is taking place over two to six years. This change in the calculation of Medicare Advantage payment limits will lead to reductions in many benchmarks.

(see glossary defining benchmarks and the Appendix for further explanation)

However, the Health Reform Law increases benchmarks based on plan quality. Plans with at least a 4-star rating on a 5-star quality rating scale will receive an increase in their benchmark. New plans or plans with low enrollment may also qualify for a benchmark increase. Also there is a provision that varies plan rebates based on quality.

If a Medicare Advantage plan obtains a rating less than a 4-star, chances are that these Medicare Advantage plans' premiums will go up. So as you evaluate Medicare Advantage plans, you might look into what their star rating is.

There are a couple YouTube videos that

might be helpful in learning more about the Obamacare impact. They are from two different perspectives. One person from a citizens advocacy group entitled his video Affordable Care Act Explained, Part 6 – Medicare, http://www.youtube.com/watch?v=78N8vYfuavU. It runs a little less than six minutes. Another person talks about Medicare Advantage Plan Reductions for 2014, http://www.youtube.com/watch?v=_OUgO1xwUL0. It runs for approximately 20 minutes.

APPENDIX

So how do these plans obtain funding for your Medicare Advantage coverage?

Although somewhat complicated to most of us, Medicare pays a fixed, or capitated amount for your care every month to the insurance companies offering Medicare Advantage plans. Since recent legislation has addressed the Medicare Advantage program costs specifically, some detail about the funding of Medicare Advantage plans might help you in providing some understanding, whether you are in agreement with these changes or not.

Medicare determines Medicare Advantage funding amount based on an insurance company's annual plan bid in relation to a benchmark.

A bid represents the plan's estimated funds needed for providing the required Medicare Part A and Part B services to an average Medicare beneficiary in the respective service area (county or counties) that the plan serves.

The benchmark is the maximum amount Medicare will pay a plan in that respective service area.

Medicare is currently phasing-in new

blended benchmarks based on a percentage of a base amount as required by the recently passed/signed Health Reform Law. As some have predicted, this Health Reform Law will have the effect of reducing Medicare payments to Medicare Advantage plans.

The phase-in schedule that started in 2012 for these new benchmarks varies up to six years depending on the size of the benchmark reduction, with a longer phase-in schedule for areas where there are larger benchmark decreases.

Since Medicare Advantage revised funding is in this phase-in period, Med-Pac explains in a document dated October 2015, how the current Medicare Advantage program payment system works. If you are interested in this level of detail, you can download the document by going to MedPac's website, http://medpac.gov/documents/payment-basics/medicare-advantage-program-payment-system-15.pdf?sfvrsn=0

The bottom line is that the Health Reform Law will definitely cut payments to Medicare Advantage plans. The likely effect will be to increase Medicare Advantage premiums to beneficiaries and/or reduce some of their extra benefits. Perhaps some Medicare Advantage plans will eventually choose not to participate in the Medicare program.

GLOSSARY

BENCHMARKS

The benchmark is a bidding target for Medicare Advantage private insurance companies. Generally, Medicare updates the local benchmarks each year by the national growth rate in per capita Medicare spending.

COBRA

The Consolidated Omnibus Budget Reconciliation Act (COBRA) gives workers and their families who lose their health benefits the right to choose to continue group health benefits provided by their group health plan for limited periods of time under certain circumstances such as voluntary or involuntary job loss, reduction in the hours worked, transition between jobs, death, divorce, and other life events. Qualified individuals may be required to pay the entire premium for coverage up to 102 percent of the cost to the plan.

COVERAGE GAP

Medicare calls this stage of your Part D benefit when there is a gap in prescription drug coverage. It sometimes is called a "donut hole". For instance, in 2016 calendar year, the coverage gap is reached when your total drug costs (what you and your plan pay) reach $3,310. You then pay a portion for your prescriptions out-of-pocket until entering the Catastrophic Stage. This is when your total out-of-pocket costs, including the annual deductible and copayments/coinsurance, reach $7,062.50, then coverage begins again. Each state offers at least one plan that provides partial or full coverage during the coverage gap.

CREDITABLE COVERAGE

Your employer or union drug coverage is expected to pay, on average, at least as much as, Medicare's standard prescription drug coverage.

CRITICAL ACCESS HOSPITAL (CAH)

A small hospital with no more than 25 beds, usually in rural areas that provides limited outpatient and inpatient services. Medicare pays a CAH on a reasonable cost basis.

ENROLLMENT PENALTY

An extra amount added to your premium for not enrolling when you first become eligible for Part B and Prescription Drug Coverage. Also if you are not eligible for premium free Part A, there is a penalty if you do not buy it when you first become eligible. These penalties continue as long as you pay the premiums.

EXPLANATION OF BENEFITS (EOB)

A notice from Medicare that gives you a summary of your medical and prescription drug claims, and your costs.

EXTRA HELP

A Medicare low-income subsidy to help people pay Medicare prescription drug plan costs, like premiums, deductibles, and coinsurance.

Guaranteed Issue

A requirement that health insurance companies must permit you to enroll, regardless of health status, age, gender, or other factors that might predict the use of health services, such as pre-existing conditions. Except in some states, guaranteed issue does not limit how much you can be charged if you enroll.

Medicare Advantage (MA)

This is Part C of Medicare. It includes hospital and medical insurance, and most often includes prescription drug coverage. Some call this Medicare Alternative because private insurance companies, not the Federal Government, provide the coverage. These insurance companies must be approved by Medicare and must follow the Medicare guidelines.

MEDICARE SUPPLEMENT

If you have original Medicare you can buy additional private insurance to help pay for deductibles, co-insurance, copayments, and other health care costs that Medicare does not cover, depending on which plan you buy. You cannot use nor can you be sold this type of insurance if you are in a Medicare Advantage Plan.

MEDIGAP

This is another term for Medicare Supplement.

NATIONAL BASE PREMIUM

The amount Medicare uses to determine the late enrollment penalty for beneficiaries signing up for a Prescription Drug Plan. In 2016 this monthly premium is $34.10.

Patient Assistance Programs (PAPs)

Certain drug manufacturers that offer assistance programs for people with Medicare drug coverage that meet certain requirements.

Plan Bid

Medicare Advantage private insurance companies submission to Medicare for covering an average, or standard Medicare beneficiary. It includes plan administrative cost and profit.

Pre-existing Condition

A health condition that has existed prior to applying for a health insurance policy, or enrolling in a new health plan. It can be something as common and as serious as heart disease, high blood pressure, cancer, or diabetes, asthma, or a relatively minor condition, such as, hay fever or a previous accidental injury.

PRESCRIPTION DRUG PLAN (PDP)

This is Medicare's prescription drug benefit, or called Medicare Part D. It is a Federal Government program, which subsidizes the costs of prescription drugs and prescription drug insurance premiums for Medicare beneficiaries. It was enacted as part of the Medicare Modernization Act of 2003.

PRIMARY CARE PHYSICIAN (PCP)

The physician you see first for most health problems. He or she makes sure you get the care you need to keep you healthy. He or she also may talk with other specialist physicians or health care providers about your care and refer you to them.

SPECIAL ENROLLMENT PERIODS (SEPS)

A period of time that allows Medicare beneficiaries to sign up or make enrollment changes, outside of the initial enrollment periods, without incurring enrollment penalties.

STAR RATING

Medicare Advantage plans are rated how well they perform by assigning a star from 1 (poor) to 5 (excellent).

STATE HEALTH INSURANCE ASSISTANCE PROGRAM (SHIP)

A state program where you can obtain personalized health insurance counseling about choosing coverage at no cost. The Medicare and You booklet on the back page provides contact information for your area.

STATE PHARMACY ASSISTANCE PROGRAM (SPAP)

Many states have SPAP's that help certain people pay for prescription drugs based on financial need, age, or medical condition. Each SPAP makes its own rules on how to provide drug coverage to its members. To find out if there's an SPAP in your state and how it works, call your State Health Insurance Assistance Program (SHIP).

Resources

There are many resources on the Internet that are available to explain all of the aspects of Medicare. In doing my research for this book I used many of these various helps, explanations, and blogs. I have listed some of those resources here for your reference. Many of them go into much greater detail than I did. Depending on how much information you need and want, and the research one wants to do, please click on these websites for more Medicare information. Or do a web search on any of the topics in the book for additional information.

CMS (Centers for Medicare & Medicaid Services)

MLN (Medicare Learning Network)

Healthcare Town Hall (perspectives on healthcare reform)

JAMA (Journal of the American Medical Association)

Medicare (official U.S. Government Site for Medicare)

Medicare Blog (the official blog for the U.S. Medicare Program)

Medicare Interactive (Medicare Rights Center)

MedPac (Advising the Congress on Medicare Issues)

Social Security (United States Social Security Administration)

ABOUT THE AUTHOR

Edward Norris has been married to his wife, Kathleen for 50 years. They have three sons and five grandchildren. Although retired from the day-to-day employment duties in the medical insurance industry, he still enjoys helping people make sound decisions as they join up with Medicare. In his free time he keeps active with golf, biking, kayaking, and of course, helping the wife with gardening and yard work.

Thank you for reading. It is my sincerest hope that this guides you through the process more easily. Please visit Amazon.com to leave a helpful review for others. For any additional questions you might have, and to get up to the minute revisions, visit MediGapDecisions.com.

www.ingramcontent.com/pod-product-compliance
Lightning Source LLC
Chambersburg PA
CBHW060943040426
42445CB00011B/978